Way to Go!

To

_____

From

_____

Date

_____

Way to Go!

Way to Go!

HOWARD BOOKS
A Division of Simon & Schuster
NEW YORK LONDON TORONTO SIDNEY

Our purpose at Howard Books is to:
•*Increase faith* in the hearts of growing Christians
•*Inspire holiness* in the lives of believers
•*Instill hope* in the hearts of struggling people everywhere

Because He's coming again!

Published by Howard Books, a division of Simon & Schuster
1230 Avenue of the Americas, New York, NY 10020

Way to Go! © 2006 by Howard Books

ISBN 13: 978-1-58229-564-0
ISBN 10:   1-58229-564-6

10   9   8   7   6   5   4   3   2   1

HOWARD is a registered trademark of Simon & Schuster, Inc.

Manufactured in China

For information regarding special discounts for bulk purchases, please contact Simon & Schuster Special Sales at 1-800-456-6798 or business@simonandschuster.com.

Contributors: Gary Myers, Debbie Webb, Mary Hollingsworth
Edited by Philis Boultinghouse
Cover design by Terry Dugan Design
Interior design by Stephanie D. Walker
"A Friend in Time" is based on a popular forwarded e-mail.

Scripture quotations not otherwise marked are taken from the *Holy Bible, New International Version ®.* Copyright © 1973, 1978, 1984 by International Bible Society. Used by permission of Zondervan. All rights reserved. Scripture quotations marked NLT are taken from the *Holy Bible, New Living Translation,* copyright © 1996. Used by permission of Tyndale House Publishers, Inc., Wheaton, Illinois 60189. All rights reserved.

Contents

Wow!

Affirmation

Yesterday

Treasure

Opportunity

Gratitude

Outstanding

! Success

CHAPTER 1

Wow!

Accomplishments, fulfilled dreams, unexpected awards, quantum "life leaps"—they're all reason to celebrate with a heartfelt *wow!* And here's a wish to get your celebration off to a big start:

May God bless you and keep you.

May he multiply your endeavors and fill up your "joy reservoir."

Wow! You did a great job! May God use this happy event to remind you of his presence—and continual goodness—in your life.

Way to go!

IT IS TIME FOR US
TO STAND AND CHEER FOR THE DOER,
THE ACHIEVER, THE ONE WHO
RECOGNIZES THE CHALLENGE
AND DOES SOMETHING ABOUT IT.

Vince Lombardi

CELEBRATE
WHAT YOU WANT
TO SEE MORE OF.

Thomas J. Peters

● Learning to Read ●

To Jodi, the letters all ran together on the page. Sometimes she could distinguish between them, sometimes she couldn't. Lowercase *p*'s, *b*'s, and *d*'s really confused her, not to mention *m*'s and *n*'s. Even *i*'s and *t*'s could get inverted. But with *w*'s and *v*'s, she could never make a distinction. Why did learning to read have to be so difficult?

Ever since she could remember, Jodi had wanted to read. Her mother read books to her several times a day, her daddy read to her at bedtime, and her older brother, Jase, read her "chapter books." That was the most impressive thing of all to Jodi: Jase could read "chapter books." She had no greater aspiration in life than to read like that.

Six-year-old Jodi Spencer had been enthralled with books as a toddler, and her fascination had increased over time until it had become an obsession. Her bedroom was a testimony to her love for books. There were books on her dresser, books in her closet, books by her bed, books on shelves lining her walls. Jodi kept a stash of books in the backseat of the car and in the purse that dangled off her arm. She made sure that she never got caught in a situation where there were no books.

The fact that most of Jodi's books were storybooks with more pictures than words hadn't mattered to her until she entered first grade. She had memorized the ones her family read to her time and time again. She kept those priceless treasures on a special shelf near her bed and dragged them out when she needed a little boost in her spirits. She loved the feeling of the carefully crafted words rolling off her tongue, usually in rhyme. But in the hidden places of her heart, Jodi harbored an intense longing to be able to grasp the words with her eyes and her mind from off the page, rather than from her memory. She ached to consume and comprehend entire books without having any help and without that stuttering feeling in her head.

That was the best description Jodi had for what happened inside when she tried to read. The letters seemed to get cluttered and congested, and she felt a stuttering sensation that clogged her brain with confusion.

Jodi's mom had met with her teacher on several occasions to discuss the dilemma. Twice, a teacher whom Jodi had never seen before came to her class and took her to a small room for some special tests to determine what the problem might be. Jodi sensed their concern, but she refused to be discouraged. Jodi would go home every day and crawl up on her bed with one of the books she had memorized and "read" until her heart was content.

All of Jodi's classmates were reading by now—some slowly, some exceptionally well—but all of them were reading. Eventually Jodi caught on to the fact that she was the only one in the class who wasn't, and it was breaking her heart. She felt a heaviness in her spirit that was taking a toll on her enthusiasm for learning.

The Spencers contracted a tutor who specialized in reading disabilities. She was a very nice lady, but she and Jodi couldn't seem to nail down the problem. Her patience with Jodi helped her feel better, but after three months of tutoring, her reading hadn't improved. The tutor stopped coming.

Eleven-year-old Jase Spencer loved his little sister. She had always had such a joyful way about her. And Jase especially loved her generosity and compassion. She was very thoughtful of him. When her doctor would give her a sucker, she would always ask, "Can I have one for my brother?" In fact, if she couldn't get him one, she would save hers for him. She especially loved to buy him gumballs when she went with her mother to the grocery store and had coins to spend.

Jodi often came into his room to console him when he was in trouble with Mom or Dad. She would sneak in when they weren't looking, bringing a Popsicle or a book to read to him. She would speak tender words to bolster his fragile male ego and rub his back as she spoke, unaware that she was contributing a vital element of strength to his self-esteem. It was an intuitive response born of love and admiration. Jodi revered her big brother.

Even at his young age, Jase knew that Jodi's way with words was unique. Her verbiage reflected her passion for words. He was sure that she would be a poet or a novelist. She derived such delight from putting phrases together like puzzles, each word fitting snugly against the one before it with some twist that connected each to the other. She strung thoughts together with ease and impressive skill.

One night as Jase was passing Jodi's room in the hallway, he heard a whimpering sound seeping out from under the door. He walked in softly and discovered his little sister facedown on her bed, surrounded by her books, weeping.

"Jode," he started, "what's wrong?"

"Oh, Jase, I'm never gonna learn to read, am I?" Jodi sobbed.

Jase's heart wrenched. He had ventured that same question a couple of times when overhearing the sober discussions his parents whispered behind her back. "Sure you are, Sis," Jase responded. "With some kids it just takes longer than others, but you will read. I guarantee you that."

"How can you be so sure, Jase?" Jodi begged.

"'Cause I'm your brother, and nobody knows you like I do," he replied assuredly.

"But, Jase, my teacher has tried to help me, Mom and Dad have tried, and that tutor tried. Nobody can help me, Jase. I'm scared I'm never gonna read." Jodi broke into a wail at those last words, the despair in her heart giving full expression.

"Yeah, but I haven't tried yet, Jodi. And there's nothing I can't do," Jase said in his most confident tone of voice. "I'm fixin' to start helping you, and you're gonna read."

Now that the words had come out of his mouth, he had no choice but to act on them. Besides, he knew his determined little sister. She was relentless when she wanted something, and there was nothing she wanted as badly as she wanted to read.

"Jase, really? I mean, do you really think you can do it?" Jodi's voice was hopeful.

"Yep!" Jase said. "In fact, let's get started."

"Should we start with one of these books?" Jodi asked.

"Nope!" Jase responded. "We're gonna use one of my books."

Jase disappeared into his room and returned with one of his favorites, *The Adventures of Hank, the Cowdog*. Jodi's eyes lit up! It was a chapter book!

Night after night, Jase and Jodi stole away into one of their rooms and pored over old Hank, the cowdog, and his comical adventures. Word by word, they labored, reading and rereading—over and over. Weeks went by, then months. Some nights the two of them laughed so hard at the antics of the redneck canine that they forgot they were working; other nights they got so frustrated over Jodi's difficulty that they would end up yelling at each other and she would run to her room in tears. Jase would weary of the work, but Jodi nagged him with his promise, reminding him that he "guaranteed" that she would read.

Finally, one day just after spring had dawned, Jase and Jodi called their mom and dad into the den for a special surprise. Jodi sat perched on a stool, dressed in her favorite outfit. Her long, curly hair was pulled back into a neat ponytail, a look she thought resembled a librarian. Her big brown eyes glistened with excitement.

Jase donned a red cape, a black hat, and a sword, which doubled as a magician's wand in this case. He began with a tap on the wooden floor. "Ladies and gentlemen," Jase shouted, "it is my distinct privilege to present to you tonight the incredible Jodi Spencer! Take it away, Jode!"

At that, Jodi pulled *The Adventures of Hank, the Cowdog* out from behind her back and flashed it for her audience to ogle. Complimentary gasps came from Mom and Dad, who thought some magic trick was to follow—the book would disappear, something amazing would fall out of it, or whatever else their children's imaginations might conjure up.

Instead, she opened the book, and with an air of confidence unequaled in her experience, Jodi Spencer began to read. At first her parents thought she was reciting yet another book; after all, her little mind was like a steel trap. They were impressed, but this was nothing new. Yet after a few pages, they began to realize that this was not mere memorization. No, Jodi was reading. Really reading! When she finished the first chapter, she looked up at her audience. Jase was beaming, but tears were streaming down her parents' cheeks. "What's wrong, Mama?" Jodi asked with concern in her voice.

"Oh, honey," her mom responded, "Daddy and I are so proud of you. Way to go, Jodi! You are the best six-year-old reader I've ever known!" At that she ran to Jodi and hugged her tightly, kissing her little cheeks over and over. Her dad joined them in an exuberant embrace.

"Mama, Jase taught me!" Jodi exclaimed.

"Way to go to you too, Jase!" their dad said, reaching to bring him into the celebration. "You've helped your sister learn the most important skill she'll ever acquire."

It was an incredible evening in the Spencers' home, one they never forgot. And Jodi read three full chapters before she tired of her performance. Her teacher was elated as well when she repeated the demonstration for her whole class. They all applauded her!

Jodi Spencer never tired of reading, but more importantly, she never forgot the love of her big brother, who sacrificed so much for her sake.

Love can accomplish things that expertise cannot. And those who love enough to believe in others should always be congratulated for doing so.

DREAM LOFTY DREAMS,
AND AS YOU DREAM,
SO SHALL YOU BECOME.
YOUR VISION IS THE PROMISE
OF WHAT YOU SHALL AT LAST UNVEIL.

John Ruskin

Wow!

Affirmation

Yesterday

Treasure

Opportunity

Gratitude

Outstanding

! Success

CHAPTER 2

Affirmation

How much brighter the world would be if we filled it with yesses rather than noes. Your life is a visible affirmation of all that can be accomplished through determination, perseverance, hard work, and faith.

In saying "Way to go!" let me add a resounding "Yes!" to the new happiness that has come your way.

It couldn't have happened to someone nicer.

CONSISTENT, TIMELY ENCOURAGEMENT
HAS THE STAGGERING MAGNETIC POWER
TO DRAW AN IMMORTAL SOUL TO
THE GOD OF HOPE.
THE ONE WHOSE NAME IS
WONDERFUL COUNSELOR.

Charles Swindoll

● You Must Not Quit ●

When things go wrong, as they sometimes will
When the road you're trudging seems all uphill
When the funds are low, and the debts are high
And you want to smile, but you have to sigh
When care is pressing you down a bit
Rest if you must, but don't you quit.
Success is failure turned inside out
The silver tint of clouds of doubt

And you never can tell how close you are

It may be near when it seems so far

So stick to the fight when you're hardest hit

It's when things seem worse

That you must not quit.

Author Unknown

I *know* that there
is nothing
better for men than
to be HAPPY and
do *good* while they *live.*

Ecclesiastes 3:12

WAY TO GO!

EVERY MAN'S LIFE
IS A FAIRY TALE,
WRITTEN BY GOD'S FINGERS.

Hans Christian Andersen

*W*ow!

*A*ffirmation

*Y*esterday

*T*reasure

*O*pportunity

*G*ratitude

*O*utstanding

! Success

CHAPTER 3

Yesterday

As you take a few moments to bask in the warmth of your success, take time to recall some of your favorite or not-so-favorite memories. Think of the yesterdays when the work made you weary but determination kept your spirit strong. Remind yourself of the lessons you've learned along the way. Laugh at the mistakes that helped you grow. Bring to mind stories of your triumphs and defeats. It's good to remember the good and the bad of our yesterdays so that no matter how high you soar, you never forget where you've come from.

WAY TO GO!

Never give in, never give in,
never, never, never, never —
in nothing, great or small,
large or petty —
never give in except
to convictions of honor
and good sense.

Winston Churchill

GOD GAVE US MEMORY
THAT WE MIGHT HAVE
ROSES IN DECEMBER.

Sir James M. Barrie

• Love on the Run •

She giggled to herself as she attached the number to her shirt. In her wildest imagination she would never have pictured herself running in a marathon. She stretched while the cool morning breeze hit her face and brought her back to the task at hand. She pushed herself into the crowd, waiting to hear the starting gun.

When the shot rang out, she was on her way, a rush of adrenaline carrying her the first few miles. The hours gave her time to think. To remember. She began running because he did. At first it was a way to be together and get a little exercise. After they were married, it was a planned time to enjoy the early morning hours, as well as a way to enjoy the glow of the sky as the sun peeked above the horizon. After the first five years the early morning run became a way to stay connected. The comfortable stride they fell into became a symbol of their commitment to stay in step with each other in all areas of their lives. Sometimes a brief run in the evening air was a means to outrun the stress they dealt with as their responsibilities increased with their careers as well as the addition of the children.

She remembered the point when the goal of running became to forget. To run away. She could still hear the sound of the ambulances as she rushed into the emergency room after The Call. The day had started like all the others with a morning jog in a fine mist that had later turned into a hard rain. They had parted with "I love you" and "See you tonight." The next day she started running alone.

The early morning jog soon became a hard run to clear the fog caused by another night of listening to the clock tick and praying, "God, help me to understand. Help me to keep my faith and show it to the children like he would have wanted me to."

After months, the run became a time to remember the good things of days gone by. It was a selfish time to embrace the memories that helped her make it through the rest of the day. With the encouragement of friends and her children, the run became a time of training her body and mind for a marathon. She knew their encouragement was to train physically. She knew the real training for her was to face the race emotionally.

The roar of the crowd brought her back. She was nearing the end. Her friends would congratulate her for finishing the race. She would congratulate herself for crossing the finish line between "Why?" and "Why not?"

$\mathcal{R}un$ in such a way
as TO GET
the *prize.*

1 Corinthians 9:24

*W*ow!

*A*ffirmation

*Y*esterday

*T*reasure

*O*pportunity

*G*ratitude

*O*utstanding

! Success

CHAPTER 4

Treasure

This one moment in time is a gift from God, to do with all that you dream possible. Treasure it. Remember it. Use it as a catalyst for your future happiness.

To help savor the moment, try these ideas:

- Journal your thoughts about it.
- Record any answers to prayer in a prayer diary.
- Call a friend and share it "live."
- Bake a cake and celebrate!

IF YOU CAN DREAM IT,
YOU CAN DO IT.
ALWAYS REMEMBER
THIS WHOLE THING
WAS STARTED BY A MOUSE.

Walt Disney

● Psalm 23 ●
NLT

The LORD is my shepherd;
I have everything I need.
He lets me rest in green meadows;
he leads me beside peaceful streams.
He renews my strength.
He guides me along right paths,
bringing honor to his name.

Even when I walk
through the dark valley of death,
I will not be afraid,
for you are close beside me.
Your rod and your staff
protect and comfort me.
You prepare a feast for me
in the presence of my enemies.
You welcome me as a guest,
anointing my head with oil.
My cup overflows with blessings.
Surely your goodness and unfailing
love will pursue me
all the days of my life,
and I will live in the house of the LORD forever.

WAY TO GO!

SHOOT FOR THE MOON.
EVEN IF YOU MISS IT,
YOU WILL LAND
AMONG THE STARS.

Les Brown

Above all else,
guard your *heart,*
for it is
the WELLSPRING
of *life.*

Proverbs 4:23

Wow!

Affirmation

Yesterday

Treasure

Opportunity

Gratitude

Outstanding

! Success

CHAPTER 5

Opportunity

Opportunity often comes along when we least expect it. Sometimes we even have difficulty recognizing it when it presents itself. But if we maintain a sense of expectancy—expecting opportunity to appear at any moment—we will be ready when it knocks on our door.

You were ready. You had your eyes open and your heart in gear. When the knock of opportunity sounded at *your* door, you were standing on the edge of tomorrow, expectantly looking toward the future and all its possibilities. Way to go!

WAY TO GO!

W HATEVER YOU CAN DO,
OR DREAM YOU CAN,
BEGIN IT.

Goethe

WAY TO GO! WAY TO GO!

I ATTRIBUTE MY SUCCESS
TO THIS—
I NEVER GAVE
OR TOOK ANY EXCUSE.

Florence Nightingale

• One Is All Right with Me •

Cameras flashed, guests cheered, and music swelled as the groom wrapped the bride in his arms for a kiss. Then, bathed in a flood of warm candlelight, they strode down the flower-strewn aisle past Jean's row. The flushed, wide-eyed groom caught Jean's eye and winked. How dashing, how glowing and innocent this young couple looked, and how wonderfully curious were the circumstances that led Jean to join them this night.

It had been after school, just three weeks earlier. She was leaning over a desk helping a student with math when a sturdy young man walked in. At first Jean didn't recognize him.

"I doubt you remember me, Mrs. Maxwell," he said, "but I was one of your fourth-grade students about fifteen years ago. I'm Dan Horton. It was Daniel back then."

"Well, let me look at you, Daniel," Jean said, scrutinizing him with interest. "Yes, Daniel! I remember you. It's so good to see you again. Has it really been fifteen years?"

"I'm afraid so," Dan said, pleased she'd remembered him.

"Well, look at you, all grown up and so handsome. A far cry from that scruffy little boy I remember. Let's see . . . weren't you . . . I seem to recall one or two incidents with you and another boy . . . what was his name?"

"Taylor. Taylor Vincent," Dan said, grinning sheepishly.

"You two were a couple of rascals. Didn't you pull the fire alarm once and hide out in the boys' room?"

"Yes ma'am. That was us."

"Well . . . Daniel," Jean chuckled. "How nice of you to stop by and see me. What brings you back to Emerson Elementary?"

"I'm getting married in a few weeks," Dan said nervously. "This may sound a bit strange," he continued, "but I was wondering if you would do me the honor of attending my wedding. It's here in town, so you wouldn't have to travel."

"Getting married? That's wonderful! Who's the lucky girl?"

"Her name is Kelly-Grace Lockhart." Jean noticed Daniel's warmth when he spoke of his future bride. "We met in college. She's good for me. Keeps me in line."

"That must comfort your parents," Jean chuckled.

"Yes ma'am, it does," Dan grinned. "Listen, I know you've got work to do here," he said, reaching for an envelope in his jacket, "but here's an invitation. That's my penmanship on the front. As you can see, it's still pretty much the way you left it."

"Yes, I see that." Jean feigned disapproval.

"The wedding's in three weeks—on Saturday night. It would really mean a lot to me if you'd come."

"I'll see what I can do," Jean promised.

"Great!" Dan grinned and waved over his shoulder as he headed toward the door.

"Oh, and Daniel," Jean called after him.

"Yes ma'am?" Dan asked politely, stopping in the doorway.

"Let's have no pranks at the altar."

"No ma'am." Dan chuckled. Then he was gone.

In the twinkle-lighted reception hall, Jean found a place at the end of the receiving line and waited her turn.

"I'm Jean Maxwell, Daniel's fourth-grade teacher," Jean said, as a perky bridesmaid reached out her hand in greeting.

"Oh, Mrs. Maxwell! How great of you to come! Dan

was so hoping you'd be here! I'm his sister, Shelly."

"Nice to meet you, Shelly. It was a lovely wedding."

"Wasn't it? Mrs. Maxwell, you may remember my parents. Mom and Dad, you remember Mrs. Maxwell."

Dan's mother clasped Jean's hand warmly. "We're so honored that you came. You did so much for our son."

"Well, I'm glad to hear it, though I really don't guess I did anything special."

"We'll chat a bit later," Mrs. Horton promised, smiling. "I'd like you to know how important you've been to our son."

When the bride and groom's first dance was announced, Jean sat down at the nearest table. *What a dazzling bride*, Jean thought, as she watched the couple embrace. *Daniel has found quite a winner*.

After the dance Jean felt a tap on her shoulder.

"Mrs. Maxwell. I believe you're wanted down front." Dan's father stood beside her, offering his arm.

"I'm just fine here, Mr. Horton," she said. "Really."

"This is Dan's idea," Mr. Horton said firmly. "He'd like you to sit with my wife and me."

"Oh, I couldn't," Jean protested.

"We insist."

"My goodness," Jean said, as she reached for her beaded purse and then stood and smoothed her dress. When she reached the family's table, Dan got up from his place beside his bride. All eyes followed as he walked toward Jean, cradling a bouquet of creamy-white Eskimo roses.

"These are for you, Mrs. Maxwell," Dan said with a broad smile.

"What in the world?" Jean asked with growing wonder.

"I know it's a little unorthodox," Dan said solemnly, "but it's my wedding, and I want to do this. I want you to know what you've meant to me."

"I'm speechless," croaked Jean, her throat tightening with emotion at the unexpected appreciation. "Thank you so much."

"Thank you, Mrs. Maxwell . . . for everything!" Dan said with feeling. "I'll never forget you."

"You're welcome, son," Jean said, tears glistening in her eyes. "For whatever it was," she added softly, as Dan returned to his bride.

"Mrs. Maxwell," Dan's mother said. "Please, sit down. It's obvious you have no idea what this is all about."

Jean shook her head. "Will somebody please tell me?"

"You were the only teacher who ever believed in Dan—

who ever saw his heart and his potential," whispered Dan's mother. "Whenever he got in trouble—which we both know was often enough—you would take that opportunity to tell him, 'Daniel Horton, you're a better man than this. You can't fool me. I see good things in you. What's the big idea of pretending to be some kind of hoodlum? Now go wash your hands, get to the head of that line, and march us out to the playground like the leader you were born to be.' Mrs. Maxwell, other than you, none of Dan's teachers had patience with him."

"I'm so sorry," Jean said, shaking her head again as Dan's mother continued.

"Year after year his teachers either ignored or belittled him. One or two even mocked him in front of the class." The pain was still evident in Mrs. Horton's eyes. "We know he wasn't the easiest student to teach," she admitted. "But when Dan was about fourteen, he started saying things like, 'I'm so stupid. Everybody hates me. I don't blame them; I hate me too.' By the time he was sixteen, the situation had gotten so bad that he went to a nearby bridge, fully intending to jump."

Dan's mother's eyes glistened as she reached for Jean's hand. "And do you know what kept him from going through with it, Mrs. Maxwell?"

"My goodness, no. What?"

"You did," she announced, pausing to let Jean fully absorb the impact of her statement.

"What . . . ?" Jean exclaimed, confused.

"Dan told us later that, as he prepared to kill himself, he remembered you and your faith in him. Somehow he believed you'd be disappointed if he gave up. He couldn't bear the thought of disappointing the one person who really believed in him, so he didn't jump. So now, on the most important day in his life, Dan wanted to share it with the person who made the rest of his life possible."

Jean's mind raced in a million directions at once. *I can't believe this. Can it be true that I've played such an important role in this young man's life? How could anything I did ever make such a difference? What if I had failed to touch this boy's higher nature? How many other students are in desperate need of love and encouragement? Am I using my position of influence as an opportunity to do all I can for all the Daniels in my class this year?*

"Thank you for telling me, Mrs. Horton," was all Jean could think to say aloud as she struggled to maintain her composure.

Driving home, Jean had to pull her Buick to the side of the road. She sat there for a long time. When she wasn't wiping her eyes and blowing her nose, she thought about her life, her teaching, and what she'd learned that evening.

When she got to school on Monday, Jean did exactly what she'd done every day for thirty years. She put her coffee on the side table, plopped some graded papers on her desk, and opened her lesson book. Then she folded her hands on the crease in the page and said aloud, "Father, help me use this day as an opportunity to make a difference in some child's life. Just one is all right with me."

Next, Jean did a new thing. She took a single white Eskimo rose out of her bag and dropped the stem in the empty bud vase at the corner of her desk. Then she got up, sipped her coffee, and in perfect cursive penmanship, wrote the math assignment for the day on the chalkboard.

LIFE AFFORDS NO HIGHER PLEASURE
THAN THAT OF SURMOUNTING
DIFFICULTIES, PASSING FROM ONE STEP
OF SUCCESS TO ANOTHER,
FORMING NEW WISHES,
AND SEEING THEM GRATIFIED.

Samuel Johnson

Let us RUN
with *endurance*
the *race* that GOD
has *set* before *us.*

Hebrews 12:1 NLT

*W*ow!

*A*ffirmation

*Y*esterday

*T*reasure

*O*pportunity

*G*ratitude

*O*utstanding

! Success

CHAPTER 6

Gratitude

A heart that makes room for gratitude is never disappointed. The blessings we bestow on others have a way of boomeranging back to us—sometimes in unexpected ways, but always there nonetheless. An attitude of gratitude equips us to face both the mountains and the valleys of life, because we know that when we trust the journey to God, everything we encounter contributes to our ultimate good.

May your happiness be complete as you give thanks for the good things he has brought your way.

WAY TO GO!

GRATITUDE IS BORN
IN HEARTS THAT
TAKE TIME TO
COUNT UP PAST MERCIES.

Charles E. Jefferson

THE UNTHANKFUL
HEART . . . DISCOVERS NO
MERCIES; BUT LET THE
THANKFUL HEART SWEEP THROUGH
THE DAY AND, AS THE MAGNET
FINDS THE IRON, SO IT WILL FIND,
IN EVERY HOUR,
SOME HEAVENLY BLESSINGS!

Henry Ward Beecher

• A Friend in Time •

Todd and Troy had been friends since the seventh grade. Todd, a gifted athlete, stocky and strong, was walking home from school one Friday when he saw the thin-framed Troy toting at least seven books and various items from his locker. Todd was thinking about all the activities he had planned for the weekend when he saw a group of boys come upon Troy with mischief in their eyes. They poked fun at the seemingly studious boy, knocked the books from his arms, and then ran away.

Todd, always troubled at the sight of injustice, ran to help Troy up. "Hey, my name is Todd; what's yours?" Todd said cheerfully.

"Troy is my name," came the glum response.

"Don't worry about those guys; they're a bunch of jerks. I've had a few run-ins with them myself," Todd said sympathetically. "You know, there are other things to do on the weekend besides homework. There are football games, parties, or just hangin' out with friends."

"Well, I don't have too many friends," Troy said as he walked away.

Todd caught up with him and stood in front of him. "Well, you have one now, Troy. I'll walk you home, and then we can go to the football game tonight and hang out all weekend. How does that sound?"

"I, uh, guess it sounds all right," Troy said haltingly.

The boys did spend that weekend together and every weekend after that all through high school. They participated in life together in every way two boys who are growing a union of souls can. Troy helped Todd in classes he didn't understand, and Todd helped Troy learn some basic athletic skills, which were difficult for the physically weaker boy.

They shared the heartache of being turned down by the girls they wanted to take to their first prom. They shared the hurt of losing a friend in an auto accident and staying up all night to pray and ask God to help them understand the loss. And they celebrated the day they got their driver's licenses by trading off the driving responsibilities every hour on the hour, all weekend long.

As graduation approached, they realized they would not be going to the same university. Troy, graduating with top honors in his class, had a full ride to a top-level institute for learning in the East, and Todd would be going to a state university to save money. They spent their last weekend together reliving the pains and the pleasures of their shared friendship.

Along with the top honors, Troy would be giving the valedictory speech to the whole assembly on Thursday night during the graduation ceremonies. Todd tried to get Troy to practice his speech on him, but Troy would simply say, "You will just have to wait, my friend."

As the proceedings began, anticipation filled the air for both young men. In so many ways, this night was the beginning, yet it also was the conclusion of the life they had grown accustomed to. The school principal stood and introduced Troy with well-deserved accolades.

Troy came to the microphone and began with a stammer in his voice. "On this day of congratulations and celebration, I want to express my deepest gratitude and appreciation to one particular friend—Todd Adams. Would you come up here and join me, Todd?" A visibly stunned Todd stood slowly and walked up the aisle to stand right next to Troy.

Troy began with emotion in his voice. "Todd doesn't know it, but he is the reason I stand here today. Six years ago Todd Adams met me on the street. My arms were full of books, and my heart was full of hurt and anxiety. He befriended me on the very day I needed a friend the most. You see, I wasn't just on the way home with an armload of books. I was on the way to take my life, and I had emptied my locker so my mother wouldn't have to do it after they found my body."

Gasps were heard from all over the auditorium. Both boys, eyes brimming with tears, faced each other. Troy put his hands on Todd's shoulders, looked him squarely in the eyes, and said, "You see, my friend, you did not simply save my weekend on that fall afternoon in seventh grade—you saved my life. It is because of you that I stand here today. Thank you, Todd. Thank you with all of my heart for being the truest of friends. What you saw that day was a boy in need; what I found was a hero of the highest order."

Todd and Troy did go to different universities, but theirs was a friendship that lasted a lifetime. They walked arm in arm through life just as they had done through their school years. Each was afforded many opportunities to be a hero to the other, and both rose to the occasion every time.

Give *Thanks* to the LORD *Almighty*, for the LORD is GOOD; his *love* *endures* forever.

Jeremiah 33:11

WAYTOGS

Wow!

Affirmation

Yesterday

Treasure

Opportunity

Gratitude

Outstanding

! Success

CHAPTER 7

Outstanding

Accomplishments don't always receive the praise they deserve. Frequently our devoted time and hard work go unnoticed and unappreciated. After all, working hard is just a part of life. But this time your efforts can't be overlooked. I am proud of you. You've done your best and it shows.

Two thumbs up, a round of applause, a standing ovation. It needs to be said: You've done an outstanding job.

CIRCUMSTANCES ARE JUST RAW
MATERIAL OUT OF WHICH GOD MAKES
CHARACTER AND STRENGTH AND
VIRTUE. ONLY THROUGH EXPERIENCE
OF TRIAL AND SUFFERING CAN
THE SOUL BE STRENGTHENED, VISION
CLEARED, AMBITION INSPIRED,
AND SUCCESS ACHIEVED.

Helen Keller

WHAT WE ARE IS
GOD'S GIFT TO US.
WHAT WE BECOME
IS OUR GIFT TO GOD.

Eleanor Powell

• The Upside-Down Letter •

Marcus was seven years old and African-American. He lived in what writer Anne Rivers Siddons called the "treacherous South," in a time when racism was served up at Southern tables like cornbread and dumplings.

It was time for the annual Christmas program at the local elementary school. Marcus was cast as the holder of the *T* in the letter lineup that spelled out MERRY CHRISTMAS. Sharon Andrews won the coveted role of Mary, the mother of Jesus. To the aggravation of her brothers and sisters, she made a nightly ritual of posing and primping in front of the mirror in the costume her mother had made her. Then she'd spend the rest of the evening shushing her brothers and sisters as she rehearsed in the living room until bedtime. As the day of the scheduled performance approached, her brothers and sisters tired of her movie-star behavior and were eager to get the play over with. Sharon's mother, Betty, worried that her children would be so annoyed with Sharon that they would miss the whole meaning of the Christmas drama.

The night of the program arrived, and the weather was bitterly cold and snowy. Betty bundled her five children up and headed to the school. "Why do we have to go?" "How long will it last?" "Do we have to hug Sharon after it's over?" "Mama, don't let them talk when I'm onstage!" Betty fielded her children's comments for the duration of the ride to what should have been one of the most meaningful nights of the holiday season. *How can I turn this night around and make this a night they will remember for more than Sharon's attitude and the bad weather?* thought Betty.

Sharon was whisked off to put on her costume as Betty and her other children found seats in the middle of the auditorium. The curtain opened to twenty-five brave children, all decked out as shepherds, wise men, angels, and an assortment of barnyard animals. They struggled through their lines but managed to bring the familiar story of Christ's birth to life. Sharon did perform splendidly. All her practice paid off, and as much as they hated to admit it, her siblings were truly proud of her. They applauded loudly as Sharon took her bow.

It was now time for the finale, the string of youngsters

spelling out the seasonal greeting. This was Marcus's big moment. But unbeknownst to him, his letter was upside down. The audience roared, finding his mistake incredibly amusing. But Betty was shocked at the behavior of the audience and hushed her children, who had also begun to snicker. Betty's heart went out to Marcus as his face melted into a mask of humiliation. The laughter came because of his letter being upside down, but he thought they were laughing at him—because he was black. The laughter went on too long, and the boy was close to tears.

As the curtain closed, Betty motioned to her children to follow her, and they all quickly disappeared through a side door next to the stage. Thinking they were being hurried off to congratulate Sharon, the children looked everywhere for their sister.

"There she is, Mama," one of the children said.

"We'll see her in a minute," Betty said as she made her way through the maze of children and parents.

Puzzled, the children followed their mother right up to the little boy who sat waiting in the wings for his parents. Betty bent down until she was eye-level with Marcus and gently took his hand. She spoke in a strong and encouraging voice: "You did a wonderful job out there. I want you to know that the audience wasn't laughing at you. They were laughing at your letter. It was turned upside down." Betty picked up the letter and showed Marcus the problem. "You, Marcus, were outstanding."

Sharon had looked around until she found her family surrounding her classmate. She joined them as they congratulated Marcus on his performance. Realizing the importance of the moment, she, too, bragged on the grateful little boy. A smile slowly formed on Marcus's lips, and he thanked them all. Betty had done it. She managed to make the night a night to remember, especially for a little boy named Marcus.

I will *praise* you,
O *LORD*,
with *all* my HEART:
I will *tell* of
all your *wonders*.

Psalm 9:1

*W*ow!

*A*ffirmation

*Y*esterday

*T*reasure

*O*pportunity

*G*ratitude

*O*utstanding

*! S*uccess

CHAPTER 8

Success

Success is born of effort and inspiration, hard work and conviction, dedication and passion.

Though the road to success will inevitably be strewn with obstacles, it is those who push ahead with determination and unwavering faith who achieve the goal. Congratulations to you on your success!

May you always invest your heart wholly in all you do and raise your hand to God in praise for his blessings of success in your life.

THERE IS WONDERFUL
FREEDOM AND JOY
IN COMING TO RECOGNIZE THAT
THE FUN IS IN THE BECOMING.

Gloria Gaither

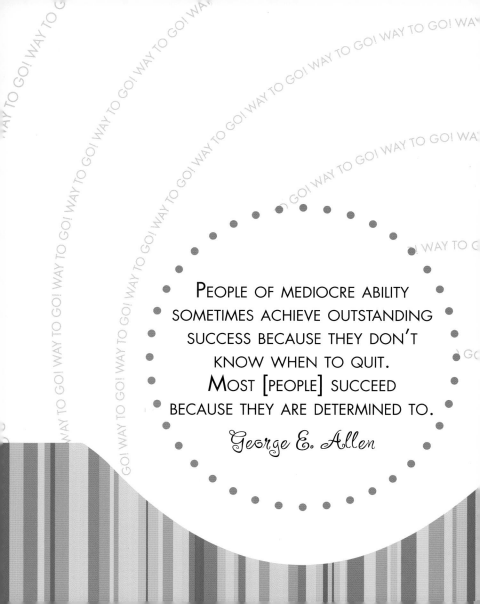

PEOPLE OF MEDIOCRE ABILITY SOMETIMES ACHIEVE OUTSTANDING SUCCESS BECAUSE THEY DON'T KNOW WHEN TO QUIT. MOST [PEOPLE] SUCCEED BECAUSE THEY ARE DETERMINED TO.

George E. Allen

• The Willow Tree Party •

The year Melinda turned eight, she accomplished an incredible feat. She climbed the willow tree in her backyard. Climbing a willow tree certainly wouldn't seem that significant except that this tree was huge. It was gargantuan. It was a kingdom waiting to be conquered. It rivaled the tree of *Swiss Family Robinson* fame.

Melinda's mother had raised all of her children with a long tether. She never minded if they roamed the woods or swam in the pond. She would shake her head when Melinda came home with bloody knees or poison ivy, but she never said, "You'd better stay away from there." No, without knowing it, Melinda's mom taught her that a fertile imagination was more important than good grades in school—though Melinda managed to get both.

Being a tomboy meant Melinda participated in her share of death-defying feats in the woods behind her house. There she fought battles on hilltops, crossed streams on fallen logs, and scaled cliffs by clutching large roots that stuck out from the red clay.

One afternoon, as the sun was beginning to set, Melinda came tromping out of the woods for supper. She spied that gargantuan willow tree. There it stood—just inside the clearing of her backyard—close to the woods but not part of it. Its "willowy" limbs draped to the ground, forming a fort underneath where anything could hide. The trunk was stout, and Melinda reasoned that someone had planted it years ago. Melinda stared at the tree, almost daring it to call her name, challenging her to conquer it.

She had climbed willow trees before, but not this one. The branch closest to the ground had been too high for her seven-year-old legs. But today she was eight, and the thought entered her mind that maybe, just maybe, she was taller now and could reach that branch and enter the private home of the willow tree.

Melinda walked up to the trunk and strained to grasp the first branch. It was still too high, so she jumped. No luck. She jumped again. This time she grabbed the branch and hung on for dear life, only to feel her hands scrape the bark on her way down. Not ready to admit defeat, she got back up and only briefly glanced at her skinned knees and scuffed red tennis shoes.

An idea formed in Melinda's head. Many times she

had seen her daddy tote water in a large metal bucket. The bucket sat in a corner of the garage, covered with cobwebs. But a few cobwebs had never stopped Melinda, and she decided it was time to put that bucket to good use.

She dragged it out to the backyard and positioned it on the most level spot she could find beneath the willow tree. One foot, then two feet. She felt the bucket wobble. But just before it turned completely over, she grabbed the branch and managed to pull herself into the "green room."

There she was at last, sheltered by the green curtain of leaves, with no one but herself to extend congratulations for her monumental success. The wind blew softly, making the curtain rustle. She lay back on the wide branch and relished the quietude of a lazy summer day. It was a wonderful and glorious feeling.

She was eight years old.

It was her birthday.

She had done it!

The *God*
of HEAVEN
will *give* us
success.

Nehemiah 2:20